The Motherless Mother's Guided Journal

The Motherless Mother's Guided Journal

PROMPTS FOR REMEMBERING AND CONNECTING WITH
MOM THROUGHOUT THE PARENTING JOURNEY

Melissa Pennel

FOLLOW YOUR FIRE PUBLISHING

Melissa Pennel / Follow Your Fire Publishing
FollowYourFireCoaching.com
Sacramento, CA.

Ordering Information:
Quantity sales: Special discounts are available on quantity purchases by corporations, associations, and others. For details, contact the publisher at the address above.

The Motherless Mother's Guided Journal: Prompts for Remembering and Connecting with Mom Throughout the Parenting Journey —1st ed.

Paperback ISBN: 978-1-956446-21-0
Hardcover ISBN: 978-1-956446-22-7

This journal is not a substitute for professional counseling or mental health services. Please contact an organization below or one local to you for more support. Also see appendix of mental health resources on page 132.

SAMHSA (Substance Abuse and Mental Health Services Administration)
SAMHSA.gov

NAMI (National Alliance on Mental Illness)
NAMI.org

This journal belongs to ....

I am the daughter of ....
MOTHER'S NAME

She is the daughter of ....
MATERNAL GRANDMOTHER'S NAME

I am the mother of ....
CHILD'S NAME

....

....

....

....

May this journal symbolize the unbroken
connections between us

More Journals by the Author

The Questions You'll Wish You Asked:
A Time Capsule Journal Series

After losing my mom before asking her important questions, I created a journal series to write down stories, wisdom, and advice for our children.

A Time Capsule Journal for Mothers & Daughters
A Time Capsule Journal for Mothers & Sons
A Time Capsule Journal for Fathers & Daughters
A Time Capsule Journal for Fathers & Sons
A Time Capsule Journal for Parents & Children
A Time Capsule Journal for Grandparents
A Time Capsule Journal for Treasured Mentors &
Important Relationships

Write down stories for your kids.
Ask questions of your family.
Your future self will thank you.

———

The Motherless New Mother's Pregnancy Journal:
Prompts, Practices and Affirmations to Guide the Mom
Who Is Missing Her Own

———

Advice She Actually Wants: Messages for the
Pregnant New Mom from Loved Ones
(Journal for Guests at Baby Showers, Mother's
Blessings, & Women's Circles)

———

The Book Lover's Companion: Personal Reading Log,
Book Review Prompted Journal, and Book Club Guide
(Version for Kids & Teens Available)

———

Learn more at FollowYourFireCoaching.com

~For the motherless mothers~

*May you feel supported, guided,
and reminded that you are not alone on this journey.*

*A mother holds her children's hands for
a short while, but their hearts forever*

•●•

UNKNOWN

Contents

A Note to the Motherless Mother

When my mom first died, someone suggested that I pull out a photo of her, light a candle, and write to her as if she would read my words. Though I was deep in the grief of early loss and ignored most well-intentioned advice, I decided to try this practice.

I'm so glad that I did.

As I wrote the words I wish I'd spoken and filled her in on my current life, I felt an inner coil of grief begin to unwind. I repeatedly turned to this practice on my grief journey, and when I became pregnant with my first child it became a lifeline; journaling was where I'd ask for my mom's guidance, pause and sit in stillness, and wait for inner answers to emerge.

This practice (and others) became the Motherless New Mother's Pregnancy Journal: Prompts, Practices and Affirmations to Guide the Mom Who Is Missing Her Own. The journal you now hold is the follow up to that: a place to support motherless mothers further down the parenting road. These pages provide a place to record memories of mom, acknowledge important milestones and tender parenting moments, and also a space to write any other messages that you long to share with only her.

If you don't have many memories of your mom, consider asking friends and family these questions about her life. If that's not possible, feel free to skip those questions and trust that her guidance already rests within you, making up the very cells of your being. Take what works, leave what doesn't, and use this as a space to weave threads between your mom, your children, and your memories.

As I've navigated this road as a motherless mother, there is one thing I've come to believe wholeheartedly: our mothers are not absent from our parenting journey, no matter how long they've been gone. They live within us, even as our longing for them exists there as well. Having a space to acknowledge this coexisting truth is the reason for this journal. May these pages be a space for warm reflection, remembrance, and release. May they remind you that you already have everything you need to be a wonderful mother. May they nurture the faith, hope, and love that connects you to every mother everywhere, including to your own, forever.

With Love,
Melissa Pennel

HOW TO USE THIS JOURNAL:

Suggestions, Rituals, & Ideas

Treat this journaling space as a special portal — a unique way to thread connection between your mom, your children, and your wisest self. The following pages contain ideas for how to do that.

Suggestions, Rituals, & Ideas

The purpose of this journaling space is threefold: it's a means to approach the grief and love you still hold for your mom, a place to thread intergenerational legacy and connection, and a way to trace the breadcrumbs your mom left behind for your own parenting journey.

When sitting down with this journal, consider the following section guides (and how you're feeling that day.)

- If you're looking for ideas on how to thread connection between your mom and your kids, or how to incorporate and honor your mom during big moments, consider the "Life Practices and Rituals" at the end of this section.

- When you want to remember your mom and document memories, turn to the "Mom's Life & Memories" section. (This is the only section where you write *about* mom, rather than to her.)

- If you feel moved to see connections between your journey and your mom's, flip to the "Mom's Influence: How You Shaped My Parenting" section. (In this section you are journaling to mom.)

- When feeling emotional about a milestone or important date for you or one of your kids, consider journaling in the

"Milestones" section (writing to mom.)

> If things have been feeling especially hard or especially wonderful, consider writing in the "Challenges and Celebrations" section (writing to mom.)

> If you just feel like writing (or venting) for no particular reason, flip to the "Messages to Mom" pages and let it all flow (writing to mom.)

Now that you've got a practical understanding of navigating this journal, what follows are some practices that support you and deepen the tender experience that is writing to and about your mom. The most important thing is that you write freely and imperfectly, just as you would have shown up in your mom's company.

Rituals for Writing

When sitting down to write, close your eyes and attune to your breath. Recall that this same breath has continued since the moment you were placed into your mom's arms when you were just a baby. Consider that this breath has never failed you, always been with you, and is now nourishing you as a mother. Observe it going in and out, feel it expand and relax your belly, and see how it connects you to both your ancestors and yourself. Breathe at your own pace for as long as it feels nourishing, and allow that breath to form a sacred space as you begin to write.

• • •

Keep a candle nearby. When writing in the journal, light the

candle and take a few moments to watch the flame dance. Allow the light to keep vigil with you as you write within these pages, and when you're done writing, whisper a "thank you" and blow the candle out.

•●•

Find a picture of your mom and tuck it within the journal. Before sitting down to write, pull out the picture and study it. Notice the familiar curve of her mouth, eyes, and face - remember how it felt to be in her presence and in actual conversation. Ask her to join you as you write, and envision her sitting beside you, over your shoulder, watching your hand move across the page. Relax into the easy familiarity you had with your mom, and allow it to take the pressure off of writing "well" or "right." (This ritual is especially helpful for the prompts designed to consider how your mom would have advised you around a specific issue.)

•●•

Gather sacred objects to join you at your writing space. Maybe it's a rock that has always felt magical, a ring that your mom loved, or a trinket from a trip you took with her. You might burn some sweet-smelling oil, soften the lighting, and make any physical changes to your environment that signal to your body and spirit that this is a sacred time.

•●•

When finished writing, draw a bath, take a walk, or put on some comforting music. It's a tender and brave thing to journal truthfully, and it's important that you tend to yourself as you walk this path. Just as your mom cared for you when you were young, and just as you care for your own children (whatever their age), regard yourself as deserving of love, nourishment, and tending. Practice treating yourself with the love you need now and always.

Treat this journaling space as sacred. Let whatever flows through you be exactly right and always good enough. Remind yourself that you are too.

Real Life Practices to Incorporate Mom on Your Parenting Journey

On your mom's birthday...

Prepare her favorite meal, go to her favorite restaurant, or bake a cake in her honor. You can tell your kids why you're doing this and share memories of birthdays you spent with her. On these dates the prompts in the "Mom's Life & Memories" section can be especially helpful, inspiring thoughtful conversations and connection with your kids.

When you're especially missing her...

Donate to your mom's favorite charity, volunteer for a cause she cared about, or do a kindness for someone in her honor. Getting your kids involved can help build the same empathy for this particular cause, and allow them to know their grandmother (and where her heart was especially tender) in a way that weaves a legacy.

When mom is missing an important milestone...

Consider recognizing your mom on days or events that she would have been a big part of were she still alive. It might be as a toast you give during a reception, an honorary place setting or empty chair that you decorate in her honor, or in a quiet moment you have by yourself on the important day. Giving yourself this space to name and honor her absence can be a healing outlet, and something you can choose to keep private or include others in.

As you consider these rituals and create your own, remember that deep grief and great joy can exist on the same day in the same body.

Breathe in, breathe out, repeat.

Onward.

Mom's Life & Memories

WRITE ABOUT MOM

"She always loved visiting this lake..."
"I still remember the day we watched this movie and laughed..."
"We always ate peanut butter sandwiches on rainy days..."

A less-recognized part of loss is the feeling that we also lost the place to share stories about our loved one—the space to talk about a person who still occupies so much of our heart. This emptiness can be compounded by the longing many of us have for our children to know our mothers, even if they never actually got to meet. We often want to thread a connection where her absence looms: for them to know who she was as a person, her favorite things, and the values that she might've passed down if given the chance.

Herein lies the gift of journaling.

Use the following pages to record important aspects of your mom, memorialize stories, and as a sacred space to talk about someone who still lives presently in your heart and parenting journey. These prompts can inspire stories that you share with your own kids, or you might just be journaling for your own reflection. However you use these pages, allow them to be a space to turn toward memories that might otherwise exist only within.

Mom's Life & Memories

Mom's birthday: ....

Her parents' names:

....

....

Her grandparents' names:

....

....

....

....

She was born & raised in:

....

....

....

....

Things she shared about her childhood home:

....

....

....

....

....

....

Some childhood memories Mom shared with me:

....
....
....
....
....
....
....
....
....
....
....

Things she shared about her relationship with her own parents:

....
....
....
....
....
....
....
....
....
....
....
....
....

Mom's favorite foods:

....
....
....
....
....
....

Her favorite places to travel:

....
....
....
....
....
....
....

Her favorite books, movies, or TV shows:

....
....
....
....
....
....
....
....

Her favorite music:

....
....
....
....
....
....

A group or cause she cared deeply about:

....
....
....
....
....
....
....

A quality she admired in others:

....
....
....
....
....
....
....

What I know about her own pregnancy and birth:

....
....
....
....
....
....
....
....
....
....
....
....
....
....
....
....
....
....
....
....
....
....

Stories she told me about her grandparents and extended family:

....

....

....

....

....

....

....

....

....

....

....

Stories she shared about our distant ancestors:

....

....

....

....

....

....

....

....

....

....

....

She was especially passionate about:

....

....

....

....

....

....

People she loved a lot:

....

....

....

....

....

....

....

Mom's sense of humor could be described as:

....

....

....

....

....

....

....

Some of her favorite activities:

....

....

....

....

....

....

Some of her least favorite activities:

....

....

....

....

....

....

....

Something (or someone) she always made time for:

....

....

....

....

....

....

....

....

Her favorite season:

....

....

....

....

....

....

Her favorite holidays and traditions:

....

....

....

....

....

....

....

A dish she prepared on holidays or special occasions:

....

....

....

....

....

....

....

....

Something she was insecure about:

....
....
....
....
....
....

Something she was proud of:

....
....
....
....
....
....
....

A quality others admired in her:

....
....
....
....
....
....
....
....

Someone she really looked up to:

....
....
....
....
....

Something she always made time for:

....
....
....
....
....
....

She really thrived when:

....
....
....
....
....
....
....

Other stories from her life:

....

....

....

....

....

....

....

....

....

....

....

....

....

....

....

....

....

....

....

....

....

....

Our Shared Memories

Some memories of her birthdays:

....
....
....
....
....
....
....
....
....
....

Memories of my birthdays spent with her:

....
....
....
....
....
....
....
....
....
....
....
....

Some memorable trips we took together:

....
....
....
....
....
....
....
....
....
....
....
....
....
....
....
....
....
....
....
....
....
....
....
....

Traditions we shared:

....
....
....
....
....
....

Memorable holiday memories with Mom:

....
....
....
....
....
....
....

Some summer memories with Mom:

....
....
....
....
....
....
....

A point in our relationship when we struggled:

....

....

....

....

....

....

An especially close phase in our relationship:

....

....

....

....

....

....

....

An especially funny moment we shared:

....

....

....

....

....

....

....

What Mom taught me about love:

....
....
....
....
....
....

What she taught me about handling failure:

....
....
....
....
....
....
....

What she taught me about honesty:

....
....
....
....
....
....
....
....

Other life lessons she taught me:

....
....
....
....
....
....
....
....
....
....
....
....
....
....
....
....
....
....
....
....
....
....

Mom was especially cautious about protecting me from:

....

....

....

....

....

....

The most trouble I remember being in with her:

....

....

....

....

....

....

....

Something I know she was proud of me for:

....

....

....

....

....

....

....

How Mom would comfort me when I was young:

....
....
....
....
....
....

How she comforted me as I got older:

....
....
....
....
....
....
....

Ways she would care for me if she were still here (and how I
am finding that support for myself):

....
....
....
....
....
....
....

If she could see me now I think she'd be especially proud of me for: ....

....

....

....

....

....

....

....

....

....

....

....

....

....

....

....

....

....

....

....

....

....

More memories:

....
....
....
....
....
....
....
....
....
....
....
....
....
....
....
....
....
....
....
....
....

Mom's Influence: How You Shaped My Parenting

WRITE TO MOM

"I always think of you when..."
"Mom, I had no idea what this felt like..."
"Some things you taught me about being a parent..."

However old your children are, there have likely been moments on the parenting journey when you long to talk to Mom. Not to simply ask a question, though there are lots of those moments too, but to lean in and confess: *I understand this so differently now, mom.* Maybe it's potty training, your child's first day of school, or how it feels to have a child move out of the house; it can feel like walking alongside our mother in the past, but now seeing an experience from an entirely different angle.

Use the following pages to write directly to Mom about the ways you now understand the past, how she influences you in the present, and the impact of her parenting on your own motherhood journey. Keep in mind that even if you don't have memories of a certain phase, especially if she died particularly young, her influence informs the very soil within which you grew. Draw near to her there and trust in that connection.

Onward.

Ways you inspired me to become a mom:

....

....

....

....

....

....

....

....

....

....

....

Moments I have especially missed you on this parenting
journey:...

....

....

....

....

....

....

....

....

....

....

....

Things I learned about motherhood from watching you:

....
....
....
....
....
....

Things I aim to do similarly:

....
....
....
....
....
....
....

Things I aim to do differently:

....
....
....
....
....
....
....

Things I only understand now:

....

....

....

....

....

....

....

....

....

....

....

....

....

....

....

....

....

....

....

....

....

....

....

Experiences that have made me see you from a different perspective:

....

....

....

....

....

....

....

....

....

....

....

....

....

....

....

....

....

....

....

....

....

....

....

....

Something that must have been really difficult for you:

....

....

....

....

....

....

Some things you permitted that I won't allow:

....

....

....

....

....

....

....

Some things you didn't allow that I am more relaxed about:

....

....

....

....

....

....

....

....

Something about you that I now appreciate more:

....

....

....

....

....

....

A situation I'm now in awe of the way you handled:

....

....

....

....

....

....

....

Traditions you inspired me to continue or start with my own kids:...

....

....

....

....

....

....

....

Some aspects of parenting in today's world that I wonder what you'd think of:

....

....

....

....

....

Something I used to disagree with you about, but now feel similarly:...

....

....

....

....

....

....

Ways I am incorporating you and your memory on my motherhood journey: ....

....

....

....

....

....

....

....

Ways parenting has changed me:

....

....

....

....

....

....

....

....

....

....

....

....

....

....

....

....

....

....

....

....

....

....

....

....

....

When I do these things, I always think of you:

....

....

....

....

....

....

....

....

....

....

....

....

....

....

....

....

....

....

....

....

....

....

....

....

....

Milestones:
Birthdays, Graduations,
& Important Family Dates

WRITE TO MOM

"She would have loved seeing Jack walk across that stage..."
"Mom would have absolutely showered Charlie with gifts on her birthday..."
"This was the day my own adoption was final and we'd always celebrate it..."

Birthdays, graduations, and important family anniversaries are some of the big and small parts of life when we especially miss our moms. These milestones are often filled with joy and grief, excitement and reflection– emotions already present on the parenting journey, but magnified on specific milestones.

The following section is a space to reflect on your experience of these dates, while also journaling messages you might have shared specifically with mom. Remember that she still lives on within you: the following pages are a place to reflect how.

45

Dear Mom,   Date:.................

I am thinking of you because today is

....

....

....

....

....

....

....

....

....

....

....

....

....

....

....

....

....

....

....

....

....

....

....

Dear Mom,   Date:............

I am thinking of you because today is
....

....
....
....
....
....
....
....
....
....
....
....
....
....
....
....
....
....
....
....
....
....
....
....
....

Dear Mom,   Date:..................

I am thinking of you because today is
....
....
....
....
....
....
....
....
....
....
....
....
....
....
....
....
....
....
....
....
....
....
....
....

Dear Mom,   Date:.................

I am thinking of you because today is
....
....
....
....
....
....
....
....
....
....
....
....
....
....
....
....
....
....
....
....
....
....
....
....
....
....

Dear Mom,   Date:................

I am thinking of you because today is
....

....

....

....

....

....

....

....

....

....

....

....

....

....

....

....

....

....

....

....

....

....

....

Dear Mom,   Date:..................

I am thinking of you because today is
....

....

....

....

....

....

....

....

....

....

....

....

....

....

....

....

....

....

....

....

....

....
....
....
....
....
....
....
....
....
....
....
....
....
....
....
....
....
....
....
....
....
....
....
....
....
....

Dear Mom,   Date:................

I am thinking of you because today is

....

....

....

....

....

....

....

....

....

....

....

....

....

....

....

....

....

....

....

....

....

....

....

....

....

....

....

Dear Mom, Date:.................

I am thinking of you because today is
....
....
....
....
....
....
....
....
....
....
....
....
....
....
....
....
....
....
....
....
....
....
....
....
....

Dear Mom,   Date:.................

I am thinking of you because today is
....

....

....

....

....

....

....

....

....

....

....

....

....

....

....

....

....

....

....

....

....

....

....

....

....

....

Dear Mom,   Date:................

I am thinking of you because today is
....

....

....

....

....

....

....

....

....

....

....

....

....

....

....

....

....

....

....

....

....

....

....

....

Dear Mom,   Date:..................

I am thinking of you because today is
....

....
....
....
....
....
....
....
....
....
....
....
....
....
....
....
....
....
....
....
....
....
....
....
....

Dear Mom,   Date:................

I am thinking of you because today is

....

....

....

....

....

....

....

....

....

....

....

....

....

....

....

....

....

....

....

....

....

....

....

Dear Mom,   Date:................

I am thinking of you because today is
....

....
....
....
....
....
....
....
....
....
....
....
....
....
....
....
....
....
....
....
....
....

Dear Mom, Date:..................

I am thinking of you because today is
....

....

....

....

....

....

....

....

....

....

....

....

....

....

....

....

....

....

....

....

....

....

....

Dear Mom,   Date:.................

I am thinking of you because today is
....

....

....

....

....

....

....

....

....

....

....

....

....

....

....

....

....

....

....

....

....

....

....

Dear Mom,   Date:................

I am thinking of you because today is
....

....

....

....

....

....

....

....

....

....

....

....

....

....

....

....

....

....

....

....

....

....

....

Dear Mom,

Date:..................

I am thinking of you because today is

....

....

....

....

....

....

....

....

....

....

....

....

....

....

....

....

....

....

....

....

....

....

Dear Mom,

Date:..................

I am thinking of you because today is

....

....

....

....

....

....

....

....

....

....

....

....

....

....

....

....

....

....

....

....

....

....

....

....

Celebrations and Challenges: Write to Mom During Tender Parenting Moments

WRITE TO MOM

"This time is SO incredible. I wish my mom were here..."
"Things have never felt so hard. I wish my mom were here..."

There are certain seasons of life (and motherhood) that are extremely tender. These parts of our journey can be especially joyous or especially difficult, and in both places we often long for our mom's presence.

The following pages are a place to journal to your mom during these moments, and then (if you're so moved) to ask for her insight. When things are great, how might she have celebrated with you? When things are tough, how might she have reassured you? As you write and then consider your mom's possible words, remember that her love makes up the very foundation of your being. When you get quiet and consider her response, you've got more of her inner guidance than you might think.

Dear Mom,   Date:.................

I am feeling especially....................................and am thinking of
you because: ....
....
....
....
....
....
....
....
....
....
....
....
....
....
....
....
....
....
....
....
....
....
....
....

What I think you might say to me right now...

....

....

....

....

....

....

....

....

....

....

....

....

....

....

....

....

....

....

....

....

....

....

....

....

Dear Mom,   Date:...................

I am feeling especially.................................and am thinking of

you because: ....

....

....

....

....

....

....

....

....

....

....

....

....

....

....

....

....

....

....

....

....

....

What I think you might say to me right now...

....
....
....
....
....
....
....
....
....
....
....
....
....
....
....
....
....
....
....
....
....
....
....
....
....

Dear Mom,   Date:..................

I am feeling especially.................................and am thinking of

you because: ....

....

....

....

....

....

....

....

....

....

....

....

....

....

....

....

....

....

....

....

....

....

....

....

....

What I think you might say to me right now...

....
....
....
....
....
....
....
....
....
....
....
....
....
....
....
....
....
....
....
....
....
....
....
....
....

Dear Mom,   Date:.................

I am feeling especially....................................and am thinking of
you because: ....
....
....
....
....
....
....
....
....
....
....
....
....
....
....
....
....
....
....
....
....
....
....
....

What I think you might say to me right now...

....
....
....
....
....
....
....
....
....
....
....
....
....
....
....
....
....
....
....
....
....
....
....
....
....
....

Dear Mom,   Date:..................

I am feeling especially.................................and am thinking of

you because: ....

....

....

....

....

....

....

....

....

....

....

....

....

....

....

....

....

....

....

....

....

....

What I think you might say to me right now...

....
....
....
....
....
....
....
....
....
....
....
....
....
....
....
....
....
....
....
....
....
....

Dear Mom,   Date:..................

I am feeling especially................................and am thinking of

you because: ....

....

....

....

....

....

....

....

....

....

....

....

....

....

....

....

....

....

....

....

....

What I think you might say to me right now...

....
....
....
....
....
....
....
....
....
....
....
....
....
....
....
....
....
....
....
....
....
....
....
....

Dear Mom, Date:................

I am feeling especially...................................and am thinking of

you because: ....

....

....

....

....

....

....

....

....

....

....

....

....

....

....

....

....

....

....

....

....

....

What I think you might say to me right now...

....
....
....
....
....
....
....
....
....
....
....
....
....
....
....
....
....
....
....
....
....
....
....
....

Dear Mom,   Date:.................

I am feeling especially...................................and am thinking of
you because: ....

....

....

....

....

....

....

....

....

....

....

....

....

....

....

....

....

....

....

....

....

....

What I think you might say to me right now...

....
....
....
....
....
....
....
....
....
....
....
....
....
....
....
....
....
....
....
....
....
....
....
....

Dear Mom,   Date:.................

I am feeling especially.................................and am thinking of

you because: ....

....

....

....

....

....

....

....

....

....

....

....

....

....

....

....

....

....

....

....

....

....

What I think you might say to me right now...

....
....
....
....
....
....
....
....
....
....
....
....
....
....
....
....
....
....
....
....
....
....
....
....

Dear Mom,   Date:................

I am feeling especially...................................and am thinking of

you because: ....

....

....

....

....

....

....

....

....

....

....

....

....

....

....

....

....

....

....

....

....

....

....

What I think you might say to me right now...

....

....

....

....

....

....

....

....

....

....

....

....

....

....

....

....

....

....

....

....

....

....

....

....

....

Messages to Mom:
Write to Mom Just Because

WRITE TO MOM

Sometimes the only person we long to talk to is our mom, and for no special reason... we just miss her. Use the following pages for any messages, requests for support, or to simply vent (like you might've done when she was still here.) Allow your words to flow freely, your writing to be imperfect, and simply talk to your first friend, first love, and first teacher....your mom.

 Afterword

Dear mama,

I hope this journal has been a reminder that your mom is still here to support you on your parenting journey.

She's in the breath you draw in and out - the same breath she once checked for in the middle of the night, lying her hand gently on your tiny chest as you slept.

She's in the tear that runs down your cheek - tears much like those she once shed on her own motherhood journey.

She's poured into your very foundation: an influence that might not always show, but whose presence loved you into being. The same being that now nourishes your own kids and shows up to this beautiful life you've created since she left.

Return to this space whenever you most need comfort and guidance, and please share this journal with other motherless moms who might need the same.

And in case no one has told you lately: You are doing such an incredible job, mama. Just look at you, and all you've been through.

Your mom would be so proud of who you have become.

With love,
Melissa Pennel

Mental Health Resources

Mental health is always important, and there are tools to support you on your journey. Use the below resources as a starting point to finding support locally. You are not alone and there is help.

SAMHSA (Substance Abuse and Mental Health Services Administration)
Website: SAMHSA.gov
Phone: 1-800-662-HELP (4357)

NAMI (National Alliance on Mental Illness)
Website: NAMI.org
Phone: 1-800-950-NAMI (6264)

National Suicide Prevention Lifeline
Website: suicidepreventionlifeline.org
Phone: 1-800-273-8255

For New Moms:

Postpartum Support International
Website: Postpartum.net
Phone: 1-800-944-4773

About the Author

Melissa Pennel is a mother, life coach, and author. She believes in the healing power of words, that motherhood is sacred, and that everyone is a writer if given the right prompts. She lives in Northern California with her partner, children, and beloved cats.

Find more of Melissa's work at FollowYourFireCoaching.com.

This journal is in memory of her mother,
deLise Rae Cline-Pennel.

www.ingramcontent.com/pod-product-compliance
Lightning Source LLC
Chambersburg PA
CBHW051628120626
46551CB00014B/1993

* 9 7 8 1 9 5 6 4 4 6 2 1 0 *